W9-ACH-482

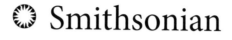
Smithsonian

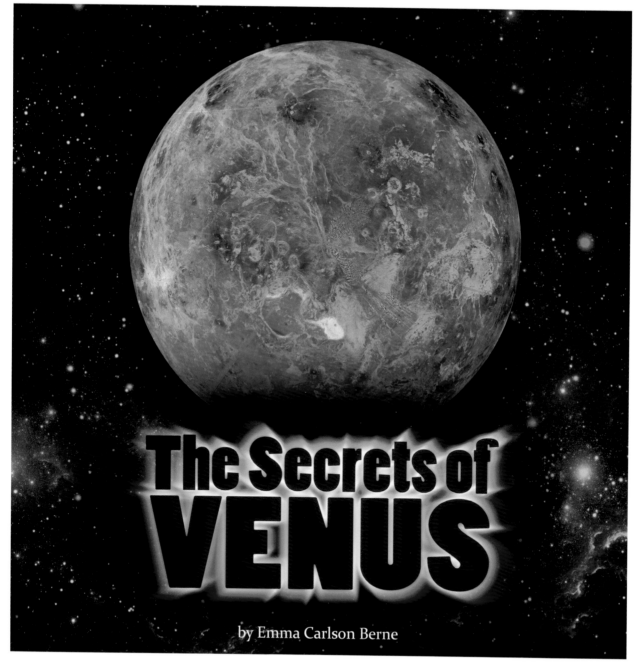

The Secrets of
VENUS

by Emma Carlson Berne

CAPSTONE PRESS
a capstone imprint

Capstone Press
1710 Roe Crest Drive, North Mankato, Minnesota 56003
www.capstonepub.com

Library of Congress Cataloging-in-Publication Data
Berne, Emma Carlson, author.
 The secrets of Venus / by Emma Carlson Berne.
    pages cm. — (Smithsonian. Planets)
 Summary: "Discusses the planet Venus, including observations by ancient cultures, current knowledge of Venus, and plans for future scientific research and space exploration"—Provided by publisher.
 Audience: Ages 8-10
 Audience: Grades 2 to 4
 ISBN 978-1-4914-5870-9 (library binding)
 ISBN 978-1-4914-5903-4 (paperback)
 ISBN 978-1-4914-5914-0 (eBook PDF)
1. Venus (Planet)—Juvenile literature. 2. Venus (Planet)—Exploration—Juvenile literature. I. Title.
 QB621.B42 2016
 523.42—dc23   2014046197

Editorial Credits
Elizabeth R. Johnson, editor; Tracy Davies McCabe and Kazuko Collins, designers; Wanda Winch, media researcher; Tori Abraham, production specialist

Our very special thanks to Andrew K. Johnston, Geographer, Center for Earth and Planetary Studies, National Air and Space Museum, Smithsonian Institution, for his curatorial review. Capstone would also like to thank Kealy Gordon, Smithsonian Institution Product Development Manager, and the following at Smithsonian Enterprises: Ellen Nanney, Licensing Manager; Brigid Ferraro, Director of Licensing; Carol LeBlanc, Senior Vice President, Consumer & Education Products; Chris Liedel, President.

Photo Credits
Bibliothèque Nationale de France: Gallica, 10; Black Cat Studios: Ron Miller, 13, 15; ©Calvin J. Hamilton, 11; European Space Agency, 25 (top), 27 (bottom), AOES/Medialab, 27 (t); Lunar and Planetary Institute, 5 (bottom); NASA, 23, Courtesy of Adrian O'Campo, 25 (b), JPL, cover, back cover, 1, 5 (back), 16, 29, JPL-Caltech, 28; Science Source, 8, 21, SPL, 7, Walter Myers, 17, 19; Shutterstock: anekoho, 9 (right), nienora, space background, Vadim Ermak, 9 (left); Wikipedia: Adamt, 6

Direct Quotations
Page 25 from NASA Solar System Exploration profile, solarsystem.nasa.gov/people/

Printed in Canada.
032015   008825FRF15

Table of Contents

Mysterious Beauty

The planet Venus revolves 67 million miles (108 million kilometers) from the Sun. It is covered with clouds of poisonous gas and showered regularly with acid rain. But it is named after the Roman goddess of beauty.

This moonless planet is also called the Evening Star. Its brilliancy and movements have fascinated people from the Mayans to the Romans to present-day scientists. But for thousands of years, Venus kept its secrets hidden from those on Earth.

Venus is often called Earth's sister planet. It is similar to Earth in size, mass, and density.

Venus' thick cloud cover makes the planet very reflective and easy to spot in the night sky.

Fast Facts

Distance from Sun: 67 million miles (108 million km)

Diameter: 7,521 miles (12,104 km)

Moons: 0

Rings: 0

Length of day: 243 Earth days

Length of year: 225 Earth days

Venus

Earth

Deity in the Sky: The Mayans and Venus

The Mayan people have lived in what is now Mexico and Guatemala for thousands of years. The ancient Maya were skilled astronomers. They tracked the movements of the Sun, the Moon, and Venus. They kept records on bark-paper books called codices between 1800 BC and 900 AD. The Mayans even built buildings with the observation of Venus in mind.

Today we know that Venus orbits the Sun every 225 Earth days. The ancient Maya didn't have this information. They tracked the movement of Venus through the night sky. They discovered a different cycle that lasted 584 days.

At specific times of the year, the Mayans linked the movements of Venus to bad luck and violence.

Mayan codex

Phases of Venus

As Venus and Earth orbit the Sun, Venus moves through our night sky in phases. These phases are caused by sunlight reflected off Venus, toward Earth, similar to the phases of the Moon.

Phase 1: Venus appears after sunset for 250 days

Phase 2: Venus disappears for 8 days

Phase 3: Venus appears just before sunrise for 236 days

Phase 4: Venus disappears for 90 days

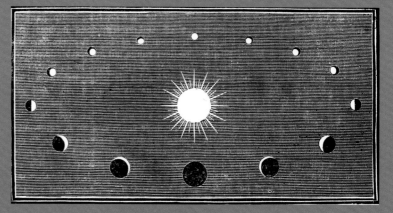

The Mayans tracked these phases and tied them to the story of the god Kukulcan. It was said that during phase two, Kukulcan died. When Venus returned to the night sky for phase three, Kukulcan was reborn.

Love and Fire: Mythology of Venus

The Mayans weren't the only ancient people to observe the mysterious Venus. The Sumerians, living in what is now Iraq, called the planet Inanna. They worshipped it as a god who could rain fire from the sky. The Aztec civilization located in modern Mexico believed that Venus could bring disaster down on the people in the form of violent storms.

Venus is the brightest object in the sky, after the Sun and the Moon.

The Romans named Venus after their goddess of love and beauty, most likely because it shines so brightly in the sky. The Babylonians also linked Venus to feminine love. They named the planet Ishtar after their goddess of women. Modern astronomy has respected these ancient beliefs. The international symbol for the planet Venus is the same symbol used for womanhood.

Venus is the only planet named for a woman. All of the features on Venus have female names, except for one. The Maxwell Montes mountain range is sometimes called "The Only Man on Venus."

From Point of Light to Planet

Ancient people knew Venus only as a moving point of light in the sky. When astronomers had telescopes to use, they realized that they were seeing a planet. The secrets of Venus were at last being decoded.

Italian astronomer Giovanni Cassini was the first to sketch the surface of Venus in 1667. He didn't realize that the beautiful swirls he observed were probably optical effects of his telescope. In fact, Venus is covered by thick clouds.

Early scientists thought Venus might be a planet suited for life. It wasn't until the Mariner 2 spacecraft flew to Venus in 1962 that we had a closer glimpse into this strange world.

Cassini's sketch

The first people to look at Venus through telescopes thought they were seeing the surface of the planet. Around the early 1900s, astronomers realized they were seeing clouds instead. It is not possible to see Venus' surface through its thick layers of clouds.

The cloud cover on Venus is very thick—anywhere from 30 to 42 miles (48 to 68 km).

Standing on the Surface of Venus

Venus is a strange and secretive planet. Its surface is hidden by thick poisonous gas. Scientists use radar to see beneath the atmosphere.

Regions of Venus' surface are pitted with volcanic craters and canyons. Some of them are huge. The crater Ishtar Terra is a lava-filled basin as big as the entire United States. The peak of the mountain Maxwell Montes is higher than Mount Everest.

Craters can remain intact on Venus for as long as 400 million years. There is no water flow or erosion to smooth them out, as there is here on Earth.

Venus may be one of the most volcanic planets. It might have more than 1 million dead volcanoes as well as a few active ones.

Many craters on Venus are filled in with old lava flows.

artist illustration of Venus' surface

The Ultimate Greenhouse

You've heard of the greenhouse effect on Earth? Well, Earth has nothing on Venus. Our neighbor is the ultimate greenhouse. Its thick, swirling atmosphere is made of 90 percent poisonous carbon dioxide. The air is very thick. Heat and moisture are trapped inside the atmosphere, close to the planet.

As a result of this heavy blanket of carbon dioxide, Venus gets pretty steamy. It is hotter than Mercury, even though Mercury is closer to the Sun. The average daytime temperature on Venus is 900 degrees Fahrenheit (482 °Celsius). Between the extreme temperature and the poisonous air, it isn't a place where humans could survive.

Venus' temperature barely changes from day to night or season to season.

It's so hot on Venus that the metal lead would melt into a liquid.

artist illustration of Venus' landscape under thick clouds

Toxic Air, Weird Weather

If you are looking for extreme weather, fly a spacecraft though Venus' atmosphere. You'll have to pass through stormy clouds made of poisonous sulfuric acid. Don't forget to brace yourself for the lightning and hurricane-force winds.

Venus' mountains are topped with snow, like mountains on Earth. But the snow is not made of frozen water. It is shiny, condensed metallic frost. The "snow" is made of metal!

Of course on Earth, rain and thunderstorms involve water. But there is very little, if any, water on Venus, except for traces of water in its atmosphere. The rain on Venus is not water rain as we know it. On Venus the rain that falls is actually made of sulfuric acid. The acid rain evaporates before it hits the surface.

artist illustration of storms on Venus

It Feels Heavy

Venus' air is dense and heavy. It creates tremendous pressure on the surface. If you have ever been deep in a pool of water, you know what pressure feels like. But if you stood on the surface of Venus, it would be like standing at the bottom of the ocean. The pressure above and around you would be so strong that you'd be crushed.

Armored spacecraft lasted only one hour on the surface of Venus. The intense pressure and high temperature destroyed them.

Venus' atmosphere is 90 times denser than Earth's.

18

artist illustration of Venus' surface

Venus' clouds are yellowish due to the large amounts of sulfur in them.

How Can a Day Be Longer Than a Year?

Venus

Not only does Venus rain acid and crush metal with just air. Our sister planet also rotates backward. On Venus the Sun rises in the west and sets in the east.

Venus is also a slow rotator. One day on Venus is the same as 243 days on Earth. But one year on Venus—the time it takes to go around the Sun—is 224 Earth days. So a day on Venus lasts longer than a year.

Uranus is the only other planet with a backward rotation. Scientists call that movement retrograde.

The cause of the retrograde motion isn't yet known. It may have been caused by planets hitting each other very early during the formation of the solar system.

Venus in transit across the Sun

Mariner and Magellan: Venus Exploration

About 50 spacecraft have been aimed toward Venus. Many have failed to reach our sister planet. Twenty missions have been successful, which is about as many as have reached Mars. The Mariner 2 spacecraft, launched in 1962, sent back reports as it passed Venus. It gave scientists their first close look at the temperatures and the lack of water on the planet.

The Magellan spacecraft launched in 1989. It orbited Venus for four years, using radar to "see" through the thick clouds. It returned images that revealed mountains, craters, and other geological features.

Venus was the first planet to be visited by any spacecraft.

Magellan eventually mapped 98 percent of Venus' surface.

The Magellan spacecraft was named after the 16th century Portuguese explorer, Ferdinand Magellan. He organized the first expedition to travel around the world.

All Aboard for the Venus Express!

Since Magellan, several other spacecraft have flown by Venus on their way to other planets. But only one other mission has orbited the planet as Magellan did. The Venus Express was launched by the European Space Agency in 2005.

The Venus Express sent back information about volcanoes, the atmosphere, and the planet's rotation. It also gathered data that proved that Venus used to have a lot of water, like Earth. The Venus Express orbited the planet for more than eight years before it ran out of fuel.

Venus Express

Scientist Spotlight:
Adriana Ocampo

When Adriana Ocampo was a little girl in Argentina, she would play "astronaut" with her dolls, and dress up her dog as her co-pilot. She didn't become an astronaut herself, but she does work with astronauts as a Science Program Manager at NASA. Ocampo coordinates different missions, including NASA's involvement in Venus Express. She says that her parents are a big reason she gets to study Venus and other planets today: "My parents were my inspiration. They always encouraged me to reach for the stars and instilled in me the knowledge that education was the gateway to making my dreams come true."

Newest News from Venus

The Venus Express sent back very exciting data. Scientists saw signs of hot lava flowing across the surface of Venus. Those signs still need to be confirmed with other observations. But if it's true, it would be a thrilling discovery. It would make Venus one of the few worlds in our solar system that has had any geological activity in the last few million years.

The Venus Express also showed that the fast winds high in the atmosphere were getting even faster over the last six years. Scientists don't yet know what that means. But since seeking answers to questions is key to science, you can be sure that they'll keep looking.

Other worlds that are geologically active are Earth, Jupiter's moon Io, and Neptune's moon Triton.

Venus Express

The Venus Express changes altitude as it orbits. In a regular orbit, it moves as close as 285 miles (459 km) from the planet's surface to as far as 39,000 miles (62,764 km).

During special experiments it has dived within 80 miles (129 km) of the surface.

For comparison, the International Space Station orbits Earth at an altitude of 250 miles (402 km).

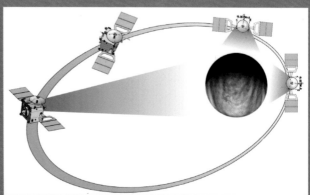

Venus Express orbiting Venus

The Future and Beyond

In the future, scientists want a mission to study the climate on Venus. One idea for a future mission is the Venus Mobile Explorer. It would look for evidence of climate change in the past on Venus. That could help us understand how climate change is happening on Earth.

Scientists want this spacecraft to be able to land on Venus and explore the surface for a long time. No other mission has done this. This future spacecraft would have to use special technology to survive the hot temperatures and extreme pressure of the atmosphere. Success with the Venus Mobile Explorer could help us uncover more secrets about our sister planet, Venus.

The Venus Mobile Explorer would have "metallic bellows"—a coil of metal that is flexible and can safely squeeze together when under pressure.

Future missions could also try to find out if Venus had oceans and how long ago they may have disappeared.

Critical Thinking Using the Common Core

1. Read the text on page 10 and look at the photograph on page 11. Why couldn't early astronomers see the surface of Venus? (Key Ideas and Details)

2. Read the text on page 22. How many missions to Venus have been successful? Why do you think other missions failed? (Integration of Knowledge and Ideas)

Index